A SPIRIT DAUGHTER
WORKBOOK

---

written by
Jill Wintersteen

FOR THE FULL MOON

Sunday, March 28th

11:48AM PST

WHY THE FULL MOON

Day becomes night, the New Moon grows into the Full Moon, and there would be no shadows without light. Our world is full of the merging of opposites, where each side could not exist without the other. Each piece of our world contains elements of something else. Just as the swirl of the Yin includes a drop of Yang and vice versa, everything in nature contains energy, which opposes the very definition of itself. Even the night includes pieces of the day shining through the light of the Full Moon and the stars. Masculine energy holds a hint of femininity, while feminine energy carries the masculine. We live in a world of integrated opposition. We also contain these opposing energies within ourselves, which require continual attention to maintain balance and harmony.

Each Full Moon brings us an opportunity to work with opposing forces within ourselves through the reflection and revelation of these energies. On the Full Moon, the Sun and the Moon oppose each other in the sky, each sitting in opposite zodiac energies. Their physical opposition forms an axis of energy, holding an array of vibrations ranging from the highest to the lowest frequencies of the signs involved. Under the light of the Full Moon, we can feel the lower vibrations, the higher vibrations, and the parts of ourselves at war with each other. This full revelation of energy is what causes a Full Moon to feel so intense. Both our light and our shadows come to the surface. We are left with the task of holding space for them to dance with each other. If we can find the strength to see all of ourselves with an open, honest heart, we then gain the opportunity to transform our energy every month on the Full Moon.

If the New Moon is the time we plant our intentions, the Full Moon is the time we do the work to manifest them. Much of this work lies in our ability to understand energies we often suppress or ignore. These suppressed energies are our shadows and hold lower frequency feelings such as anger, resentment, anxiety, and guilt, among others. Often these vibrations lie below our conscious mind and undermine our greatest efforts to create the life of our dreams. They are old patterns left over from childhood or formed during a period when we were in survival mode, just trying to get through one day at a time. Our shadows also include conditioned patterns we've used in the past to gain energy for ourselves. Until we understand that energy is infinite and always available, we naturally attempt to gather as much as we can from those around us. Our low vibrations often carry the manipulations we have used to attract attention or take control of a situation. They are our personals dramas that play out any time we want energy or attention from another.

The lower frequencies we embody directly oppose the higher frequencies needed to attract our visions. If, for instance, we hold the vibration of unworthiness, it becomes challenging to believe we are worthy of our dreams, and we will consequentially struggle to build them. If we often use anger to demand attention, it becomes difficult to build a life centered around compassion and understanding. Similarly, if we are plagued by guilt or using guilt to manipulate, then we will find it challenging to find true acceptance and belonging in our community. Our methods of controlling energy can easily be redirected once we align with higher vibrations and consciously understand that we are always connected and supported by the energy of the Universe, the energy of ourselves.

Each Full Moon brings the opportunity to align with the higher frequencies through shadow and release work. Yes, this takes work, but the Full Moon gives us the energetic boost needed to do that work. When working with lower vibrations, it's important to remember the nature of opposites. Every lower frequency you feel contains a bit of its higher oppositional frequency. Every anxious thought includes a piece of excitement, every judgment includes a bit of compassion, and every feeling of unworthiness contains a piece that understands your true value. Acknowledging the small part that stands in opposition to the lower frequency is the key to shifting your vibration under each Full Moon's light.

CREATE YOUR BALANCE

AND FIND PEACE WITHIN

LIBRA FULL MOON

Libra brings the element of air to this Full Moon. The Air signs connect us and remind us we live in a world full of other people. We are one week in Aries Season, which inspires us to focus on ourselves and our journey. The Libra Full Moon encourages us to feel where others fit into our journey and how we can form partnerships that support and nourish the life path of everyone involved. This Moon is a time to create balance and harmony in our relationships, including the one with yourself. It's a time to resolve conflicts and clearly view how past pain or trauma may be affecting today's interactions. This Libra Full Moon encourages love, compassion, and non-judgment, as we repair burnt bridges and forge new relationships that align with who we are becoming.

Ruled by Venus, Libra is the sign of the scales. This energy represents peace, balance, and justice. Venus is the planet of love and beauty that teaches us how to align with the highest vibration. Libra, at its core, wants us to connect from a vibration of love to others. This energy governs our most intimate relationships and shows us how to compromise, how to create balance in our love affairs, and how to stand firm in our boundaries when needed. Libra begins this challenge of creating harmony by first providing us tools that cultivate peace within ourselves. This Full Moon is a time to become aware of the subtle signs that occur before you are triggered emotionally. What causes you to feel anger? What causes you to feel guilt, or shame, or any other emotions of the lower vibrations? More importantly to Libra, what clues do your body, mind, and energy give you before you feel an emotion?

If we can learn the subtle shifts that occur before we lose our balance, we gain the power to maintain it by using our tools. On this Full Moon, notice when intense emotions are about to arise. Notice what happens to your energy before you are triggered. Life is unpredictable. There will always be situations that ruffle your feathers or even bring up past pain. When we become triggered, parts of ourselves that we don't understand come to the surface and act out to gain attention. These can be unconscious thoughts and emotions that need healing. If we can notice our triggers before they affect us, then we have a greater opportunity to heal them. If, for instance, your partner says something that triggers an unhealed memory from the past, how do you react? When we act unconsciously, we may blame our partner or get angry with them, placing our past pain on them. Alternatively,, we can dig into our tool kit to calm our emotional body before acting on our triggers. We can then heal, release, and create new patterns of response moving forward. Feel Libra's energy this Full Moon guiding you in releasing unconscious patterns and replacing them with conscious efforts to calm your energy.

Libra takes its lessons further this Full Moon by asking us to look at and evaluate each of our relationships. Which ones limit you? Which ones liberate you? This Full Moon is a time to define your relational space. It's a time to decide if relationships are co-dependent and full of drama or if they are balanced. In intimate partnerships, we will act out old patterns and control dramas until we do the work to free ourselves from them. We will attract people into our life who create similar experiences to our past in an effort to heal them. Sometimes, with the right partner, we do heal. Other times, we end up constantly triggered and re-inflicting the same pain on ourselves from the past. We tend to cycle through similar people in our lives until we finally understand our patterns and break free of them. We heal, and our relationships change, we attract different people, and we show up fully in our power, ready to be seen for who we are. We form healthy relationships, where both parties support and nourish each other while staying true to their life journey.

On this Full Moon, take an honest look at all of your intimate relationships. These include your romantic partners but will also include your close friends, family and even some business partners who are deeply connected to you. See how you are showing up in the relationship and how they are showing up. Are there any control dramas apparent? These appear when one person is trying to gain energy from the other in the form of manipulation. Are you ever triggered in the relationship, and how do you handle it? Furthermore, how do you each support the other's journey? Do you feel nourished and listened to, or do you feel misunderstood? On this Full Moon, do the work to explore your shadows and triggers. Find balance within yourself and bring attention to your most important relationships from this place of balance.

LIBRA MOON X ARIES SUN

Every Sun Season has its opposing Full Moon. For Aries, the sign of the Self, that Full Moon is in Libra. The Season of Aries inspires us to align with our purpose and make following it our highest priority. Aries asks us to be bold, decisive, and to take action quickly based on instinct alone. Aries reminds us that we have the power to overcome any obstacle or challenge along our way. We are our greatest asset and never need to rely on anyone or anything else because we are all we'll ever need. On the other hand, Libra teaches us that while our life's mission is of great importance, our inner peace is the highest priority. Nothing is as important as maintaining inner harmony. Furthermore, when we are energetically settled, we see clearly. Our path is drawn out in front of us, and we know the next steps to take on it. We also know what to do in the face of adversity. A true warrior is most calm in the midst of battle. Libra helps us cultivate inner peace and use it as our greatest tool during times of challenge.

Libra also teaches us that our path is that much sweeter when shared with another. The challenge, though, is staying true to our own journey while supporting another on their unique path. When in a partnership of any kind, it becomes easy to drift from our path onto theirs, and vice versa. It takes a deep awareness from both people to not only stay true to their individual purpose but to nurture each other's life mission. It becomes easier if both people involved have processed their life's mission and can articulate in a way that the other understands. As with everything in life, though, there are trade-offs. To be in a fully committed relationship, compromises are often needed and required for the partnership to thrive. Our job becomes knowing what is negotiable in our world and what is off the table. We need to pick our battles, knowing when to fight and when to go with the flow. When we do dig our heels in the sand, it needs to be from a place of harmony and gratitude for another, not from an emotional reaction.

To truly master the art of relationships, we need to understand both Aries and Libra's low vibrations. When we become aware of these frequencies within ourselves, we can shift and release them. Once free of these shadows, we can fully integrate Libra and Aries's highest vibrations to form relationships that support each other in a beautiful co-creation of each other's life journey and purpose. We learn to develop healthy relationships where each person maintains their sense of identity. Furthermore, we can respect each other's boundaries and admire them for their gifts, raising their vibration each day from a place of completeness within ourselves. To achieve a high vibrational relationship, we start by searching for and shifting the lower vibrations, which undermine our energetic unions.

Libra has two main shadow sides: indecision and passive-aggressiveness. Libra views the world as parts of the same whole, all equal. This view, although beautiful, can lead to indecision because all choices are equal. Indecision can lead to anxiety because we inherently know that time is limited, and when we fail to make choices, we delay our life and its journey. This anxiety eats away at our inner peace, disturbs our well being, and muddles any relationship until we choose to begin and move forward again. At its lowest

LIBRA MOON X ARIES SUN

point, indecision can cause us to follow someone else's choice only to find out later we are unhappy and need to realign ourselves with our path. Some relationships can survive this readjustment, while others break under the pressure and the redirection of energy.

Libra's other low side of passive-aggressiveness causes us to become manipulative as we try to control a situation without clearly stating our needs. When we align with this side of Libra, we may become stubborn, procrastinate, or even avoid people. We play games and cause drama where it is unneeded simply because we are afraid to express our true feelings. In some cases, the relationship does not hold space for us to share our emotions. These types of relationships need to be adjusted to feel safe expressing ourselves, or they need to be released. In other cases, we may have never learned how to clearly state our needs and felt that our only option was manipulation to acquire the energy we needed to feel supported in the world. If this is the case, awareness and compassion is the first step to understanding how these patterns were formed. We need to honestly look at how we gain energy from others or support through passive tendencies. To shift these behaviors, we need to become comfortable asking for what we need. Communication is key in any relationship. The more we can speak our truth firmly, but without aggression, the better off our partnership will be.

It may not happen overnight, but each of us can learn how to express our needs in a non-passive approach and receive the energy we deserve from another. Likewise, we can learn how to give energy to the relationship, so the other person feels their needs are met, and their dreams are nurtured as well. It's important, though, to understand that our main source of energy comes from ourselves and the connection we have with the Universe. The energy we gain from another is never meant to sustain us or deplete them, and vice versa. In a truly high vibrational relationship, each person is abundant with energy and gives freely while also receiving frequencies from another. It is a beautiful cycle of reciprocity where both people are connected to themselves, their purpose, and each other.

On this Full Moon, we also need to look at Aries' low sides of selfishness and aggressiveness. Aries' lower vibrations cause us to act without thinking, relying on pure instinct alone, even if it means not including others in our decision. The lowest side of Aries is pure selfishness. When we align with this side, we forget we live in a world full of other people. We put our needs first at the expense of others, and we forget the importance of empathy. We only see the world through our eyes and resist understanding it through someone else's perspective. We bulldoze our partners, not hearing what they have to say and leave them feeling unheard and not respected. We become like a bull in a china shop, causing emotional havoc everywhere we roam.

Aries' other low vibration is the aggressiveness with controlling behavior. When we align with this side, we become demanding, bossy, and overly assertive. We intimidate others by yelling or asserting our power in a dominating way. This low side of Aries comes from our own internal conflict. When we align with these vibrations, we are at war with ourselves. We project this aggression onto others and start unnecessary battles. We seek to win to make ourselves feel better, but what we really need is to resolve our internal issues, triggers, and pain before engaging with another. We need to ask ourselves what the anger is a reaction to- what is the underlying emotion? And what needs to be healed?

If we look at the spectrum of energy involved in this Full Moon, on one end, we have aggression and control. On the other end, we have passivity and indecision. None are beneficial in the realm of relationships. Think over your actions in partnerships. Do you recognize any of these patterns in yourself? Know that it's ok if you do, and you always have the opportunity to shift these vibrations. Have compassion for yourself first, and know that this Full Moon's work is to bring these shadows to light. Find the root of these behaviors and begin to shift them into the higher vibrations each sign brings us. The most challenging step of any change is awareness. Align with the Moon to see yourself fully and know that you are capable of shifting any energy within you. As you begin to vibrate higher, you'll create and attract higher frequency relationships that elevate your soul's journey.

ASPECTS

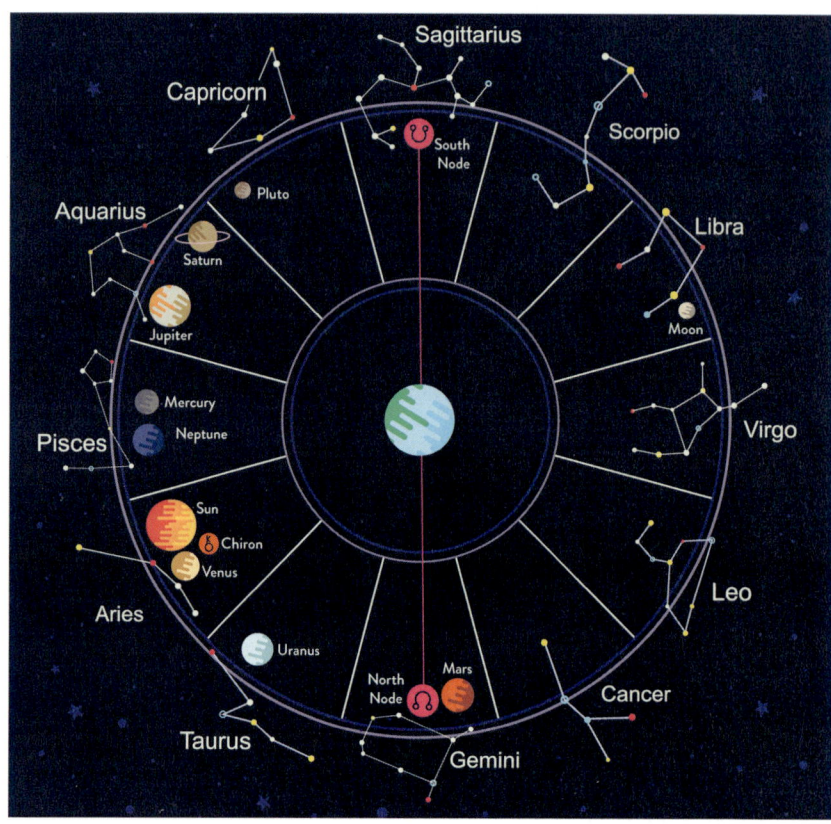

The main aspect of any Full Moon is the opposition or 180° separation of the Moon and Sun. We have a few more aspects this Full Moon that affect the day's energy and bring us different vibrations to work within our energetic body. This day, both Venus and Chiron conjunct the Sun. All three of these cosmic bodies will be at 8° Aries, combining their energy and infusing this Full Moon with their vibrations. They will all directly oppose the Moon in Libra, who is forming a Grand Air Trine with Mars in Gemini and Saturn in Aquarius. Grand Trines occur when three cosmic bodies are each 120° apart (give or take a few degrees), forming a triangle in the sky. They generally occur in the same element. This Full Moon is receiving an extra dose of air energy due to this trine.

Venus is the natural ruler of Libra and governs how we connect to love. Venus brings our attention to our heart and what we find beautiful in this world. Venus helps us find balance within our world through connecting with love. When life feels stressful, or we are overwhelmed by emotions and triggers, Venus encourages us to take a deep breath and calm down. This planet helps us feel our heart and connect to the center of ourselves, where all is stable. It also helps us connect to others who bring joy and love into our life, providing needed relief from the piles of to-do items and life pressures. The energy of Venus allows us to get lost in the feeling of being alive. It encourages us to fall in love with life over and over again, even after we've been dealt a challenging hand.

Chiron, sitting next to Venus and the Sun, is a comet. Chiron is the wounded healer in Greek mythology. Chiron was the wisest of the centaurs, whose tale was not a pleasant one. He was struck by an arrow in a "wrong place, wrong time" scenario. The wound caused by the arrow, thrown by his friend Hercules, never healed. Chiron was forced to live with his injury and his pain. Being immortal, not even death could be his relief.

ASPECTS

Chiron was a silver lining guy, though, and found ways to work around his wound. In learning to live with his pain, he was able to teach others how to accept theirs, and this acceptance healed them. Chiron's journey finally came to an end when Hercules struck a deal with Zeus, and Chiron was freed from his pain. The lesson of Chiron s story is that he suffered significant wounds in his life through no fault of his own. In many ways, Chiron was a victim, but since he was a demi-God, he never allowed himself to play the victim role. He lived with strength, wounds and all. His energy teaches us to accept our traumas as part of our life journey. They may not be pleasant, but they have made us who we are today. Once we grow to love and fully accept ourselves, our wounds can be forever healed.

Chiron brings us an opportunity for deep healing this Full Moon. This energy reveals our triggers, our wounds and illuminates our perceived weaknesses. In combination with Venus and the Sun in Aries, this vibration shows us how to connect with our hearts to heal. This healing then realigns us with our soul's journey and life's mission. This trio is a powerful force this Full Moon, opening the door for soul work at the deepest level. As they oppose the Moon, there is an opportunity for breakthroughs within ourselves that will have long-lasting positive effects on our relationships.

As you work with the energy of Chiron, Venus, the Sun, and Moon, feel how past pain shapes and molds your inner peace. What from your past disturbs your present-day peace? What old stories are triggered continually and interfere with your capacity for love and connection? What fears are leftover from your past, and how can you empower yourself not to let your past contain you? Dig deep this Full Moon and find the places you need to heal. Be honest with yourself and see how these unhealed wounds have affected your relationships. Give them love and acceptance. Share them, if it feels necessary, with those close to you, but know that no one else has the power or responsibility to heal them but you. You are capable of connecting with your heart and transforming your pain into power like Chiron. You may become a healer yourself, or you may take the lesson and apply it to your life's journey. Feel the path you are on and fall in love with your life- your whole life- this Full Moon. Fall in love with yourself and from this love attract the people who will support the highest expression of yourself.

We are also working with the opposing Grand Air Trine this Full Moon. With Saturn in Aquarius, Mars in Gemini, and the Moon in Libra, we have an abundance of air energy today. Air helps us connect to ourselves, our thoughts, our energies, and others. Air also moves quickly and allows us to shift between different energies within ourselves. Air brings us messages. It is the language of the Universe, and carries us information if we are open to it. On this Full Moon, notice what the element of Air is bringing into your life. What is moving within you? Align with Air to help you heal and transform emotions. Feel yourself connecting with different parts of yourself, integrating them as you meld different perspectives within you. As you connect different energies and emotions within, see what their combined energy helps you understand about your overall life path. Then look around you for signs and signals from the Universe. What is popping up in your world to guide you? How are the cosmos speaking to you? How do the signs you are receiving help you understand your life's bigger picture and everyone in it this Full Moon?

Continue to align with the Air element when connecting with others. What new energy can you bring into your relationships? What new ideas can you share, and how can you transform your partnerships where needed? Feel the Air around you connecting and threading you together with others. The abundance of Air this Full Moon makes it an excellent time to breathe with someone else. As you breathe in unison, you find a combined rhythm that connects your energy fields even more deeply. Work with the energy of Air this Full Moon to deepen your bonds with your most important partners. And remember, we all breathe together. What affects you, affects everyone around you. As you cultivate balance within and connect with the love in yourself, you will extend it to others and change their frequency. When you take a deep breath and calm yourself, those around you feel calmer too. We are connected in so many ways. This Full Moon brings to light some of those subtle connections and helps us nourish them.

RELATIONSHIP SCOPES

Your Sun sign is the astrological sign the Sun was in when you were born. It is the topic of most main stream horoscopes. You also have a Moon sign, which tells you the sign where the Moon was located when you were born. Your Moon governs your emotional body and tells you what your heart is here to learn in this lifetime. Look to your Moon to understand why you call certain people into your life, how you love, and what you need in a relationship. Your Moon sign also describes your reigning needs. These are the energies that make you feel fulfilled and aligned with your life. Often when you feel happy, content, depressed or angry, it is because you are either addressing your Moon's needs or ignoring them. Ideally want partners who understand, sympathize, and support your needs while understanding their own.

Below is a brief explanation about your Moon Sign and compatibility suggestions. Know that any two Moon sign's can have a happy relationship, as long as both embody their higher potential. Every energy has a low and a high side. Embodying this high side will be easiest with your "most compatible" signs. Your "opposite" Moon sign is the most reflective in pointing out lower energies and can help you shift them. These relationships can be frustrating but illuminating. Your "growth edge" Moon signs are very different in their expression of emotions. They are different from you but offer a perspective that is easy to understand. Your "greatest challenge," are signs which you may find it challenging to maintain a high vibration. It takes deep shadow and trigger work for these relationships to work, but if both parties are up for it, they can help you evolve to new, undiscovered places.

Aries Moon: Your reigning need is adventure. You are on a mission to go bravely where no one has gone before and call-in situations, which help you develop the courage to climb the tallest mountains. You are fiercely independent and seek the freedom to follow your heart at any cost. In relationships, you need someone with the same passion for life and who shares your love of adventure. You require time alone as well to pursue challenges on your own. It is best for you to have self-assured partners who give you the freedom to roam while pursuing their own passions. Your biggest trigger in a relationship is indecisiveness. You need someone who knows what they want, even if it differs from you. Confidence is key, and you'd rather debate with someone than help them vacillate between ideas. A high vibrational relationship for you consists of two people who take turns allowing the other to lead and are always up for new adventures that spice things up.

Most compatible Moon Signs: Aries, Leo, and Sagittarius
Opposites Attract: Libra (be aware of their indecisiveness)
Growth Edge: Gemini, Aquarius
Greatest Challenge: Cancer, Capricorn

Taurus Moon: Your reigning need is peace. Your heart craves steadiness in your inner and outer world. When flustered, your emotions are soothed by nature. You also need to connect with your sensory emotions to feel the world around you, including other people. You mainly rely on the language of touch to express your feelings. In relationships, you need someone who understands your need for stability and respects your comfort zones. If you feel rushed, you dig in your heels and can act like a stubborn child. You feel most comfortable with people who understand your need for peace. Drama and games are not your things. They only leave you feeling insecure and frustrated. You are honest and forthright and need someone who can meet you eye to eye in the present moment. Once you find your match, though, you commit for the long haul and even tend to stay long past the relationship's expiration date. A high vibrational relationship for you consists of two people who make each other feel secure and are comfortable getting lost in the moment together.

Most compatible Moon Signs: Taurus, Virgo, Capricorn
Opposites Attract: Scorpio (be aware of their need to psychoanalyze)
Growth Edge: Cancer, Pisces
Greatest Challenge: Leo, Aquarius

Gemini Moon: Your reigning need is to have your emotions understood. You are on a mission to express your feelings and share them with the world. Sometimes, though, you

RELATIONSHIP SCOPES

share too much before you know what it is you feel. You do best with partners who can help you sit with your feelings and understand them. Your love language is speech, and you need someone willing to have in-depth conversations with you and truly listen to your words. In relationships, you do best with people who nourish your natural curiosity about the world and enjoy exploring it with you. Steer clear of people who feel threatened or annoyed by your urge to talk to everyone you come across. You may come off a bit flirtatious, but that is not your intent. Seek a partner who is secure in themselves and encourages you to interact with those around you, and most importantly, trusts you. A high vibrational relationship for you consists of two people willing to talk through challenges with an open mind.

Most compatible Moon Signs: Gemini, Libra, Aquarius
Opposites Attract: Sagittarius (be aware of their overwhelming visions)
Growth Edge: Leo, Aries
Greatest Challenge: Virgo, Pisces

Cancer Moon: Your reigning need is to feel your heart. You, more than any of the Moon signs, need to feel. You need nourishment, and you need quiet contemplation. You also need to feel your intuition and honor it. When aligned with your intuition, you can leave the confines of your shell and be vulnerable to others. You can receive energy and give it from a place of contentment. You work best with partners who respect your need to feel and are willing to ride the waves of emotions with you. It is also important they acknowledge the inherent power of your emotions. When you have the space to feel, you instinctively make the best decisions for yourself and anyone around you. When you don't feel appreciated, or your gifts are not reciprocated, you retreat behind your fortress. You crave a connection that allows you to tear down your walls and people who appreciate the beauty held within them. A high vibrational relationship for you consists of two people willing to give and receive emotionally when needed.

Most compatible Moon Signs: Cancer, Scorpio, Pisces
Opposites Attract: Capricorn (be aware of their determined nature)
Growth Edge: Virgo, Taurus
Greatest Challenge: Libra, Aries

Leo Moon: Your reigning need is self-expression of the heart. You need to sing your song and roar your roar. Furthermore, you require a partner who supports your expression and will help you develop it through gentle encouragement. You are here to understand your worth and to learn to take up space with your presence. Once you realize that you are a true gift to everyone you meet, you will finally feel free to be yourself. In relationships, you need the freedom to express yourself, whether it be dancing around the kitchen or professing your love through generous acts of service. You need playfulness in your life and partners who can communicate this way. Steer away from people who make you feel self-conscious or belittle you. Your partner needs to make you feel like the queen or king you are and be grateful to stand in your presence. Their reward for this admiration is your loyal heart, big enough to heal the world. A high vibrational relationship for you consists of two people who cheer each other on and have mutual admiration for each other's gifts.

Most compatible Moon Signs: Leo, Sagittarius, Aries
Opposites Attract: Aquarius (be aware they don't compete for the same audience).
Growth Edge: Libra, Gemini
Greatest Challenge: Scorpio, Taurus

Virgo Moon: Your reigning need is service. You rely on logic, organization, and your skills to navigate through life. Your mission is to feel your intuition over your practical side and lean into it as your guide. Doing this will help prevent over-analysis and deep self-criticism, which you are prone to feeling. In relationships, you thrive when at service. You love to do things for others and need people who appreciate you. You also do best with partners who are organized and know where they are headed in life. While you can hold space for people to figure out their game plan, your patience quickly runs out when there is too much

You can look up your Houses at astro-charts.com

RELATIONSHIP SCOPES

fluctuation. You also do well with partners who acknowledge your emotions and help you process them. You need to feel comfortable and not under judgment to express yourself, which can be challenging for a perfectionist. At your deepest level, you are trying to heal and heal others. If you remember this and have compassion for yourself, it will help all of your relationships. A high vibrational relationship for you consists of two people who appreciate each other and are willing to share praise for each other's gifts.

Most compatible Moon Signs: Virgo, Capricorn, Taurus
Opposites Attract: Pisces (be aware not to interpret them as indecisive)
Growth Edge: Scorpio, Taurus
Greatest Challenge: Sagittarius, Gemini

Libra Moon: Your reigning need is inner harmony. Your heart needs to find peace within first, then find relationships that support this peace. You also require equality and respect. You tend to suppress your emotions through indecision. In relationships, you do best with people who bring out your true desires and inspire you to follow your heart- even if your mind is wavering. You also do well with partners who speak the language of touch, which helps you leave your head and connect with your body, the source of your inner knowing. You can debate any subject and do well with people who challenge you but still respect your opinion. Steer away from partners who belittle you or make you feel that your opinion isn't of value. Also, stay away from those who do not understand your love of beautiful things. You take pleasure in your surroundings and enjoy co-creating an environment that is energetically and aesthetically pleasing. Find someone who wants to find the perfect shade of paint with you and understands that this process is a form of meditation for your soul. A high vibrational relationship for you consists of two people who make balance and peace a priority working to create it in all aspects of their lives.

Most compatible Moon Signs: Libra, Aquarius, Gemini
Opposites Attract: Aries (be aware of their assertiveness)
Growth Edge: Sagittarius, Leo
Greatest Challenge: Cancer, Capricorn

Scorpio Moon: Your reigning need is intimate understanding. Your emotions run deep, and you like it that way. You're on a quest to understand the depths of your own subconscious. You need to first understand your inner workings, and then maybe you'll share them with another. Any relationship with you is full of intensity. When you find your match, you tend to bond for life. You love to feel you are alone in the world with your partner and are quick to create a sanctuary for you both to reveal your innermost secrets. You do not allow just anyone into your cave, though. Your walls are high, and you require a partner who respects them. Trust is important to you, and if you feel it has been broken, you become suspicious of every action and even become paranoid. If your suspicions are proven right, it's best to move on. You have a tough time recovering from betrayal. When in a healthy relationship, though, you can step into your full power and steer the ship for both of you from your deep intuitive knowing. A high vibrational relationship for you consists of two people who are willing to look at their shadows and grow together as they unravel them.

Most compatible Moon Signs: Scorpio, Pisces, Cancer
Opposites Attract: Taurus (be aware of their fear of the unknown)
Growth Edge: Virgo, Capricorn
Greatest Challenge: Leo, Aquarius

Sagittarius Moon: Your reigning need is truth. You need the freedom to roam wherever your heart desires. You know there is more to life than what is right in front of you. You also need optimism in your life, both from yourself and from others. In relationships, you bring the energy of excitement and are often the one who inspires spontaneous outings. You have a natural faith that everything will work out and require partners who have that same trust in life. You do well with people who understand your quest for adventure and can keep up with your wanderlust ways. When in a relationship, you attract serendipity for both of you. Any partner needs to acknowledge this gift and appreciate you for it.

RELATIONSHIP SCOPES

They also need to appreciate your stunning sense of humor and your ability to light up any room. Steer away from people who feel inhibited by your brilliance or resentful of the attention you often attract. A high vibrational relationship for you consists of two people who respect each other's freedom and know how to have a good time together.

Most compatible Moon Signs: Sagittarius, Aries, Leo
Opposites Attract: Gemini (be aware of their logical side).
Growth Edge: Libra, Aquarius
Greatest Challenge: Virgo, Pisces

Capricorn Moon: Your reigning need is security. Your emotions run deep, but you tend to conceal them, and need a safe space to express them. You also need solitude to understand yourself before you can trust another. Of all the Moon signs, your career plays the largest role in your emotions. To feel fulfilled, you must find work that makes you feel useful, needed, and of service. You need a purpose, and you require partners who understand this need. In relationships, you often take charge, as you know what you want and when you want it. You secretly would love to relax and allow someone else to call the shots, though, as long as they call them correctly. Work on being attracted to partners who are consistent and able to commit fully to your heart. You do not have the patience for people who flake on plans or act differently in various situations. A high vibrational relationship for you consists of two people with steady hearts and clear visions for themselves and each other.

Most compatible Moon Signs: Capricorn, Virgo, Taurus
Opposites Attract: Cancer (be aware of their emotional side)
Growth Edge: Scorpio, Pisces
Greatest Challenge: Libra, Aries

Aquarius Moon: Your reigning need is freedom. You are on a mission to find your most authentic self and stop at nothing to accomplish this purpose. You like to experiment with different methods of living and loving, which do not conform to any societal norms. You crave the chance to apply your eccentric ways to change the world and need a purpose that fulfills your heart. In relationships, you defy convention. You require partners who understand your need to dance to your own rhythm and who support each step. You express yourself through speaking and often engage in lengthy discussions about the ways of the world. You do best with someone who can keep up with your quick-witted intelligence and sense of humor. Steer away from people who are clingy or emotionally needy. You often react to these energies with aloofness and detachment, undermining the relationship. A high vibrational relationship for you consists of two people who stand in their truth, are willing to express it, and always have reverence for each other even when they disagree.

Most compatible Moon Signs: Aquarius, Libra, Gemini
Opposites Attract: Leo (be aware of their need for approval)
Growth Edge: Sagittarius, Aries
Greatest Challenge: Scorpio, Taurus

Pisces Moon: Your reigning need is expansion of the heart. You are on a mission to become one with the universe. Give yourself time and space for deep contemplation and meditation. You feel everything, including the emotions of those around you. It's important to take time to decipher which feelings are yours and which ones are another's. You require partners who understand that you are a highly emotional being and operate from a place of feeling over logic. Your intuition is strong, and with the right partner, it is nourished. When you have a partner who can meet you on a soul level, you can dive even deeper into your consciousness. If you feel you are not met at the soul level, you may become aloof and even resort to methods of escapism to hide from your feelings. A high vibrational relationship for you is two people willing to bare their soul and explore the deepest emotions without fear.

Most compatible Moon Signs: Pisces, Cancer, Scorpio
Opposites Attract: Virgo (be aware of their structured ways).
Growth Edge: Capricorn, Taurus
Greatest Challenge: Sagittarius, Gemini

LIBRA LUNAR FLOW

When we create balance in our physical body, we create balance in our emotional body. Yoga is a wonderful place to develop balance, especially between the two sides of the body. Our left side represents our feminine energy, while the right represents the masculine. Yoga brings these two physical sides into balance, and in turn, balances our energetic system. The following sequence will help move your energy and create balance in both your masculine and feminine sides. It is suggested on a Full Moon that you begin each pose with your left side, to empower it to lead since we often lead with our right side. This is the first step to bringing balance to our body's energy.

Sun Salutation A // 3 Rounds
Stand at the top of your mat. Inhale stretch your arms overhead > Exhale fold forward > Inhale lengthen out your back > Exhale step back to plank pose and lower to the ground > Inhale reach your chest up for cobra pose, legs on the ground > Exhale to Downward Dog Pose. Stay here for 5 breaths and feel your entire body expand. On Exhale, step to the top of the mat > Inhale lengthen through your spine > Exhale fold forward > Inhale come up to standing, reaching arms overhead. > Exhale hands to your heart. Pause for a moment and feel yourself centered throughout your body.

Forward Fold with Twist
Step your feet hip-distance apart > Exhale fold forward over your legs, lowering hands to the ground > Inhale lengthen out through your spine > Exhale lift your left arm to the ceiling, twisting to the left, slightly bend the right knee if needed or place a block under your right hand. Stay in this twist for 5 breaths before switching sides.

Crescent Pose with Twist
From a Forward Fold, step your right foot back into a lunge > Inhale lift your torso and bend into the front (left) knee, raising your arms to the sky. Take 5 breaths here > Exhale, twist to the left, reaching the right arm forward, left arm back. Keep your hips facing the front of the mat and breathe deeply for 5 breaths > Exhale, place your right hand down about a foot away from your left foot and reach your left arm to the ceiling. Take 5 more breaths here, lengthening your spine on each Inhale and twisting more on each exhale. Release your left hand down and step forward into a forward fold and repeat on the opposite side. Once you return to the top of your mat, Inhale as you rise to stand.

Warrior 1 > Pyramid Pose > Twisted Triangle
Standing at the top of your mat, Inhale lift your arms> Exhale into chair pose > Inhale > Exhale fold forward > Inhale lengthen through your spine > Exhale plank pose into chaturanga (elbows bent) > Inhale into Upward Facing Dog (chest lifts, hands, and tops of the feet stay on the ground) > Exhale Downward Facing Dog > Inhale step the left foot forward for Warrior 1, back foot remains flat, turning in at a 60-degree angle. Bend into the front knee and lift the arms. Remain here for 5 breaths, lengthening your torso. On exhale, lower your arms to the ground and hop the back foot in twelve inches toward your front foot > Inhale lengthen your spine as you straighten your front leg > Exhale fold

LIBRA LUNAR FLOW

over your front leg. If your hamstrings are tight, use blocks under your hands. Breathe here for 5 breaths, lengthen through the spine on each inhale, and fold deeper on each exhale. Inhale lengthen, place the right hand on a block about inside your left foot › Exhale rotate your spine to the left, lifting the left arm to the sky. Keep the hips level and feel just your spine rotating. Take 5 breaths here, twisting a little more on each exhale. Release both hands to the ground stepping back into Plank Pose on exhale and lowering into chaturanga › Inhale Upward Dog › Exhale Downward Dog. Repeat on the right side, ending back at Downward Dog.

Chair Pose › Chair Pose Twist
Return to the front of your mat. Keep your feet together and bend deeply into your knees as if you were sitting in a chair. Reach your arms upward to the sky and look up. Feel your belly drawing in, helping to direct your tailbone to the floor. Bring your hands to heart center, palms pressing › Exhale twist to the left, hook your right elbow on the outside of your left knee for leverage. Hips stay square as you twist deeper on each exhale. Feel your two sides integrating as you twist across your spine. Take 5 breaths in the twist, then return to center, forward fold over your legs for a breath. Return to chair pose and repeat the twist on the right side for 5 breaths then fold forward once again. Allow your spine and neck to fully release in this fold, holding it for 5 breaths. You may grab ahold of opposite elbows and bend your knees slightly if needed. Once you are finished, place your hands on your hips and inhale to standing.

Locust Pose Variation - 3 rounds
From the top of the mat, Inhale, reach your arms overhead › Exhale, fold forward › Inhale lengthen out your back › Exhale step back into plank pose and lower to the ground. Lay down on your mat on your belly. Have your legs hip-width apart and press into them to create stability in the lower body. Draw your belly in and feel your abs activate to support your spine. Clasp your hands behind your back, opening your chest › Inhale, lift the chest upward into a slight backbend, reaching the arms behind you. Feel as though you are creating traction through your spine as you reach the heart forward › Exhale, lift the legs, keeping them active. Reach your feet and arms back as you expand the chest forward. Take 5 expansive breaths into the back of the heart as you open the spine. Rest in between rounds for one breath, then complete the pose two more times. Slowly return to Downward Dog.

Camel Pose - 3 rounds
From Downward Dog, come up to kneeling with your legs hip-width apart. Press down into your shins and activate your abdominals. Place your hands on your hips with the fingertips going up the back, if possible. Imagine your pelvis was pressing against a wall and keep it there as you inhale to lengthen the spine upward › Exhale slightly bend back into camel. Be gentle with your back, and watch your breath. Make it smooth as you deepen the backbend on every exhale. If comfortable for you, release your head back, opening your neck. Spend about 5 breaths here then come upright slowly. Pause for a moment, then repeat, go deeper the second round.

Spinal Twist
Come back down to lying on your back. Hug the left knee into your chest and send it over the right side for a spinal twist. Reach your left arm out the side, stretching through the chest. Take 5 breaths here, then switch sides. On each Inhale, feel your back lengthen, on each exhale twist a little deeper.

Savasana
Stretch both your legs out long on the mat and place your palms facing upward in a receptive motion. Feel your entire body supported by the ground beneath you. Let your breath become natural and feel the energy circulating through you from your practice. Place your full attention on the breath moving in and out through your nose. Allow your mind to be still and your body to be calm.

LIBRA MEDITATION

The following meditation can be done by yourself to enhance your relationship with yourself or with partners. Partners can include your romantic partners, close friends, co-workers, or anyone with whom you wish to improve communication.

Eye Gazing Meditation - 3 minutes

With Yourself: Stand in front of the mirror and look yourself in the eyes. Breath deeply as you maintain the connection with yourself. Notice what emotions come up to the surface as you stare into your own eyes. Allow these emotions to express through tears or laughter, or any other sensation. Also, notice any urges to look away or any difficulties you feel when connecting with yourself. Where do they come from? What are you have trouble accepting about yourself or acknowledging? As you look at yourself with an open, honest heart, you tell yourself energetically that you accept all aspects of yourself.

With a Partner: Begin seated in front of one another in a comfortable position. Relax your eyes, but keep them open and look directly into your partner's eyes. This contact may feel uncomfortable at first but try to breathe through any feelings that may arise. Remember to stay present with your partner. Begin to breathe in sync, matching your inhale and exhale. Continue to breathe together for the entire time. Relax through your shoulders and your neck as you gaze into your partner's eyes. Feel a sense of love and compassion as you look at them and know they feel this for you. If the urge to giggle comes up, allow it, but remain fully present with the energy of the person in front of you.

Appreciation

With Yourself: Practicing gratitude is an amazing way to raise your vibration and your relationship with yourself. Take out a piece of paper or use the pages in the back of this book to write down what qualities you are grateful for in yourself. Thank yourself for the things you do for yourself and tell yourself what you appreciate most about your own being.

With a Partner: Gratitude is essential in any relationship. We often take the people closest to us for granted because they are always there. It can be easy to fall into a routine and forget how much we appreciate the other person in our life. For this practice, have a pen and paper handy. Write down "I am grateful for" then list three things you appreciate about your partner and have them do the same on their paper. On your same piece of paper, write down "I feel appreciated when" and list three things your partner does to make you feel appreciated. Once you are finished, switch papers. Take turns reading your answers out loud. For the first part, say to your partner, "You are grateful for" and repeat their list. For the second part, say, "You feel appreciated when" and repeat their answers. Then have them read your list. As you each read the other's list, listen with full presence and an open heart. Be genuinely curious about learning more about your partner.

Metta Meditation

With Yourself: Metta is the energy of loving-kindness. When we send Metta to ourselves and others, we open our hearts and raise our vibration. Sending Metta to all beings helps to strengthen your relationship with yourself and everyone you know. Begin to breathe into your heart, feeling your chest expand and contract on inhale and exhale. Think of someone you love; this can be anyone, including a pet. Feel the love you have in your heart for that person and see that person in their happiest state. As you hold this vision of them, say, "May you be happy, may you be healthy, may you be free." Now direct your attention back to yourself and feel your heart expanding. Imagine yourself in your happiest state and say to yourself, "May I be happy, may I be healthy, may I be free." Repeat this for as many people you can think of in your life.

With a Partner: Conclude your time together through a practice of Metta meditation. Close your eyes and imagine your partner in their happiest state. See them smiling and full of radiant light. Say to yourself, "May this person be happy, may they be free, may they be at ease." After a few moments of sending loving-kindness to one another, slowly open your eyes, seeing your partner fully. Thank each other for showing up to do this work together and acknowledge the bond between you.

FULL MOON SET UP

Libra is the sign of the artist, and she inspires aesthetically pleasing environments both internally and externally. Libra reminds us that our space determines how we feel internally and vice versa. If you aspire to feel calm within, then create a space that feels calm and includes elements that align energetically with the vibration of harmony and peace. Also, choose somewhere that not only includes elements of beauty but is also free of distractions. This may be a quiet location outdoors or a space in your home, which feels protected and grounded. Ideally, you want to feel at peace in your space and safe to explore the energies of the Full Moon.

Once you have your space, spend some time setting it up for your practice and Full Moon ritual. Remember, the most important piece of this Full Moon is that everything feels good to you and your energy. Include all the elements in your circle but choose colors that are soothing and inspire inner harmony. To represent Air, the element which governs Libra include auric sprays of rose water and tuberose, diffusers filled with lavender and chamomile, or smudge sticks created from juniper and sage. For the Fire element, include candles scented with rose, jasmine, or geranium. You can also choose ones filled with lavender or any other scent which brings you peace and harmony. For the Earth element, include crystals that align with both Libra and Aries. For Libra incorporate Watermelon Tourmaline, Lapis Lazuli, and Lepidolite, for Aries include Carnelian, Quartz, and Desert Jasper. Place the crystals around your space intuitively, allowing the energy of the crystal to lead you. You can also create a crystal grid in the center of the circle to move the energy for the night. For air signs, like Libra, create a spiral crystal grid with a large sphere in the middle. You can also include flowers for the Earth element and even incorporate them into your crystal grid. Roses of any kind align with the energy of Libra and can support the space with their scent and energy. Lastly, for the water element include a small bowl of silver holding some water. You can place this bowl outside after your circle on the Full Moon to charge it overnight and create your Moon Water. Cover this water and save it for your next Full Moon circle.

Once your space is set up, cleanse it with a smudge stick of your choice. Smudge in a clockwise direction, beginning at the Easterly point, moving to the South, West, North, then back to the East. Imagine a white light encasing the circle, protecting it from any external energies. Before your guests enter, cleanse each one of them with sage or palo santo, and then cleanse yourself. Once you have all entered the circle, pause for a moment to let the energy settle before you begin.

Follow your intuitive guidance when leading a circle. You can choose to practice alone or in the company of others. As a guide, begin with each member introducing themselves. Talk about the astrological energy of the day and how it is affecting each one of you. Share and learn from each other about your unique experiences with this Full Moon. Give plenty of space for each person to speak. Follow your conversation with the partner work section of this book. You can then begin exploring the rest of the practices. Do them alone, but share as much, or as little, with the rest of the group. Go over the questions and continue to learn from each other's perspectives.

Once you've finished the practices, spend some time in meditation again to allow the work to integrate into your energy. Afterward, draw some cards to help tap into your intuitive guidance. The following pages include information on card pulling and reading. Close the circle by giving gratitude to everyone who chose to honor the Full Moon with you. You can even practice writing gratitude statements on a card then passing that card to the person next to you to carry home with them. Give thanks to the elements for supporting you, to the space for existing, and for the energy of the universe guiding you along the way.

LIBRA CARD READING

Reading Cards is a beautiful way to access your intuition and tap into your, and the Universe's, higher wisdom. Anyone can pull cards, as long as you are willing to receive the information they provide. You need no prior experience, or training, just an open and clear mind.

You may use any cards you like for this practice, including but not limited to: Tarot Cards, Animal Medicine Cards, Oracle Cards or any Affirmation Cards. You also can pull cards from a few decks to gain different perspectives. If you are new to card pulling, try to ask only one deck the same question, as asking different decks the same question can become quite confusing. Below are some general guidelines on how to pull cards. Please improvise as needed and above anything else, listen to your intuition.

Clear Your Mind

A settled, grounded mind is essential for pulling cards. The last thing you want is random thoughts running around when you are trying to receive clear answers from yourself. Practice the breath work and meditation in this workbook to prepare and settle your mind. You may also clear your mind using sound frequencies through singing bowls. These can either be crystal or metal bowls. Play the bowl, or bowls, for about 3-5 minutes to help rid your mind of external noise as you focus on the harmony of the sound.

LIBRA CARD READING

Pick Your Deck

There are many different decks out there. You can choose as many as you like. Know, though, that they each provide you a different energy or medicine. Tarot Cards are the most popular and should be used carefully. Although very useful, Tarot cards can give the wrong impression if you interpret them harshly. Animal Medicine cards offer different types of messages from the animal realm which can help align with the spirit of nature. These cards give you the medicine you need to apply to your situation or question. Affirmation cards provide you with guidance in the form of words or phrases. When reading these cards, it is best to meditate on what the affirmation means for you. It is also helpful to repeat the affirmation a few times and see how it makes you feel. There are many other cards you can experiment with, like Goddess Cards, Angel Cards, and so on. The important thing to remember with any card is that they each have different angles and sides. There are often a few interpretations of the same card.

Shuffle

Shuffle the cards the easiest way for you. Some cards are smaller and can be shuffled like a regular deck of playing cards, while others with take some effort. If all else fails, spread them out on the floor in front of you then regather them. Keep a clear mind while shuffling. You can also repeat " I am open to receiving guidance and intuition." Refrain from asking your questions until the next step.

Libra Card Questions

You are free to ask the deck any questions you need answers to on this Full Moon. The following questions are meant to help you harness the energy of Libra through the cards to clarify some of these energies in your mind. This is a three-part card reading, where you'll ask the deck three questions. Before beginning, spread your freshly shuffled cards in a wide arc in front of you. Use your left middle finger to choose the card, first waving your hand slowly over the cards. You'll feel a magnetic pull, or slight tingle, in your fingertip when you hover over the right card. Chose one card at a time, taking a moment to breathe in between questions. Keep the cards flipped over until you pull all three.

What energy will help me heal and release past pain?

What energy will help me create healthy partnerships where both people are supported?

What energy will help me stay true to my path and centered in myself in relationships?

Take Them In

Once you have your cards, flip them over. Before looking up their meaning, sit with them for a moment and allow them to speak to you. Intuit your own meaning and interpretation of the card. What is the card trying to tell you? What are you trying to tell yourself? After a few moments with the cards, look up their meaning. Sit with that information, merging it with your intuitive meaning of the cards.

As with everything, enjoy this process. Do not worry if you are doing it right or wrong. Just follow your intuition, and trust the journey. Accept the cards you are dealt and use their energy wisely to help guide you when you need it the most.

We're all just walking
each other home.

-Baba Ram Dass

LIBRA PRACTICES

Relationships are fluid. They move, shift and change just like the people in them. They require awareness and the willingness to maintain them through time. Without them, though, our life would be less colorful and rich. Relationships are a fundamental part of the human experience and are something we all crave in our lives on some level. They may take work, but the right ones are always worth it.

Relationships come in all shapes and sizes. We bond with people at different times in our lives, and some people come into our world for a short time to teach us something or work out some karma. Others come into our lives for an extended period and become pivotal in our growth and evolution. An important understanding about relationships is that some are meant to last forever, while others are not. Releasing a relationship that is no longer suited for our journey can be a painful and even heartbreaking event in our life. Letting go of certain people at the right time is often needed, though, so we can move forward. Conversely, we must also recognize the relationships worth fighting for and doing the work to make them last. It can be challenging to know where to put your energy or where to back away, but your soul will always know the answer.

On this Libra Full Moon, feel into your closest relationships. Know they are all part of your soul's journey in some way, but begin to understand them at a deeper level. Feel into the ones that have taught you something important about yourself or completed a cycle of karma. Recognize that feeling of completion with some relationships and encourage yourself to thank them and release them. Then feel into the ones that are part of the long road of your soul. Decide which relationships are worth the work to maintain them because they make you a better person. Some people in our lives inspire us to vibrate higher. They don't demand it or even ask for it, but their presence alone makes us want to reach for our higher potential. These relationships support our life's mission and even help us find it.

This Full Moon is not about looking for people who complete you. You are whole already. Your first step to developing healthy relationships is to feel complete within yourself. Every relationship you have is an extension of the one you have with yourself. Once you accept, love, and know yourself, you can begin to understand which relationships support you in being more you. You can easily see which relationships come in for a reason or a brief moment in time and which ones are meant to be life long bonds. It starts, though, with feeling complete within yourself.

Know, though, that you do not need to be completely perfect, or healed, or without faults to be in a healthy relationship. Many relationships, both temporary and longer-term, bring us healing and growth. They help us change and move away from lower vibrations. The key, though, is to keep showing up for ourselves. While we may never be perfect, we do not want to make it someone else's job to heal us. They may support us in our healing journey and hold space for us to evolve, but it is always our work to unravel our shadows. A genuinely supportive partner, though, will not rush our growth or demand it. They will sit with us on our most challenging days and allow us to feel. They will also celebrate our most incredible days and be capable of genuine happiness for our accomplishments. To develop these relationships, we must accept who we are, wounds and all, and share them willingly with the right people. We must love ourselves and, from that love, attract people who will honor and uphold it.

The following practices can help you develop a higher vibrational relationship with yourself and with others. You can practice them on the Full Moon and the week after. Take your time with the questions and allow the answers to arise naturally. Know that relationship work is a lifetime journey. You can revisit these questions any time the Moon is in Libra to watch yourself grow and evolve.

LIBRA PRACTICES

---

1. Are there any relationships in your life you need to release? What have they taught you? What karma may have been worked out? And how can you have gratitude for them but still move on?

LIBRA PRACTICES

2. What does a healthy relationship feel/ look like to you?

_____
_____
_____
_____
_____
_____
_____
_____
_____
_____
_____
_____
_____
_____
_____
_____
_____
_____
_____
_____
_____
_____
_____

LIBRA PRACTICES

3. What are things you need to accept about yourself to form higher vibrational relationships in your life? Are there areas that need healing? Or shadows that need light? Or pain that needs acceptance?

LIBRA PRACTICES

4. What are some signs that you are emotionally triggered? How can you calm yourself down before you react from old patterns?

_____

_____

_____

_____

_____

_____

_____

_____

_____

_____

_____

_____

_____

_____

_____

_____

_____

_____

_____

_____

_____

_____

LIBRA PRACTICES

---

5. What helps ground you in the present moment when in communication with another? How can you keep your past out of the present and respond only to what is being discussed?

LIBRA PRACTICES

6. Libra teaches us that opposites can exist simultaneously. How can you accept and embrace different options from your partner, knowing that sometimes both of you are right? How can you see their perspective more clearly without changing your own?

LIBRA PRACTICES

7. What helps you admit what you want in a relationship? What are your priorities with bringing someone else into your life?

LIBRA PRACTICES

8. What helps you set and uphold clear boundaries with people?
Do boundaries come easily, or are they challenging for you?
What are some things that are non-negotiable even if it feels
uncomfortable to state them?

_____

_____

_____

_____

_____

_____

_____

_____

_____

_____

_____

_____

_____

_____

_____

_____

_____

_____

_____

_____

_____

_____

_____

LIBRA PRACTICES

9. Are you comfortable asking for support when you need it? Are you comfortable receiving it when given? Conversely, do you easily provide support when needed? Remember, support doesn't just include when times are tough. Supporting each other's happiness is also pivotal.

LIBRA PRACTICES

10. How easily can you express how you feel? What helps you
     understand your feelings more deeply? What helps you
     communicate them?

_____

_____

_____

_____

_____

_____

_____

_____

_____

_____

_____

_____

_____

_____

_____

_____

_____

_____

_____

_____

_____

_____

_____

_____

_____

_____

_____

AFFIRMATIONS

Write down attributes or qualities of people in your life, or in the world, that exemplify calmness and inner peace to you. These can be whole sentences describing the person or short phrases.

_____

_____

_____

_____

_____

_____

_____

_____

_____

_____

_____

_____

_____

Write down 3-5 affirmations containing pieces of the phrases you wrote about. Begin each one with "I am" and include some of the qualities you listed. Embody these affirmations each day by repeating them when you feel your inner balance become disturbed.

_____

_____

_____

_____

_____

_____

_____

_____

_____

HAPPY FULL MOON

Thank you to everyone who supported and purchased this workbook.

Special Thanks to Rebecca Reitz (rebeccareitz.com, IG:@becca_reitz) for her beautiful artwork on the cover and pages 2, 4, 6, 14, 32.

For a monthly subscription contact hello@spiritdaughter.com or visit www.spiritdaughter.com